Giotto

Giotto

Arnoldo Mondadori Arte

Texts by Stefano Zuffi

Translation by Richard Sadleir

Table of Contents

Giotto

In around 1300, Florence and the whole of Tuscany were flourishing economically and culturally: the way of life of the old city, with its simple, severe manners, was transformed by a solid, prosperous middle class of merchants and money-lenders, and the exiled Dante lamented the change through the words he put into the mouth of his ancestor Cacciaguida. It was in this context that Giotto worked so fruitfully. Of humble origins, the son of Bondone, a peasant, he fulfilled himself as man and artist in the life of the city, well aware of his social importance and the significance of the works he had left in many Italian cities in the course of his travels. His painting embodies this moral and material confidence, the satisfaction of having understood and interpreted his own time and country.

The people painted by Giotto are real men and women, with all their anxieties and hopes, their sense of wonder and human emotions. With the solid volume of their bodies they occupy a social role and a physical, tangible space in the everyday setting of town and countryside.

The greatest achievement of Italian culture at the start of the fourteenth century was the awareness of the active presence of the individual in history and the world. This period saw the first signs of that intellectual movement that, a century later, was to blaze forth in the fullness of Renaissance humanism. The new language was taking shape: the vernacular Italian used by Dante and Boccaccio, whose clear, ringing cadences matched the handling of scenes and figures in Giotto's works, and at the same time sculpture, in the works of Arnolfo di Cambio and Giovanni Pisano, also achieved its full expressive range, from vibrant animation to solemn calm.

As his contemporaries said, Giotto changed the language of art "from Greek to Latin." And yet his apprenticeship was spent in a figurative training still influenced by Byzantine art. This tradition stemmed from the Imperial court in Byzantium and was firmly rooted in all of eastern Europe: it created a tradition which regulated all the images used in a very specific code of representation. It did not aim to reproduce an impression of perceived reality, but to furnish a visible expression, through aristocratic symbolism, of celestial realities and figures. In this way the separate scenes of sacred history followed an iconographic scheme that remained unchanged and was diligently repeated by successive artists. Giotto's master, Cimabue, and his great contemporary, Duccio da Boninsegna, were still partly faithful to this attitude in painting, which was elegant and refined, with a strong linear emphasis, but their work was in other ways very different. From his earliest known works, Giotto adopted a totally different approach, and in doing so achieved one of the great breakthroughs in Western art.

It is highly likely that Giotto made a journey to Rome when still a young man, and that this stimulated him to develop his clear and personal interpretation of ancient art, seen as a model of restraint and harmony, together with a subtle and acute understanding of nature and human sentiments. The late thirteenth century artists in Rome (like Pietro Cavallini, Jacopo Torriti and Filippo Rusuti) had already begun moving in the same direction, but it was only with Giotto that this movement triumphed, soon to spread through the influence of his works in Assisi, Rome, Rimini, Padua, Naples and Milan, all stages in his progress marked by fresco cycles and other works of outstanding importance. Some of them have been lost, but they played a decisive role in creating local schools drawing inspiration from Giotto's work. Within a few decades there were schools of his followers in all parts of Italy, working with different degrees of originality: but it was Florence in particular that embraced the teaching of her illustrious son. When Renaissance painting began to flower early in the fifteenth century, with Brunelleschi, Donatello and Masaccio, Giotto was always acknowledged as its strong, enduring root.

Though it sounds like a paradox, the truth is that Giotto (like Dante) has been thought of as "modern" for over seven hundred years because he lived and acted as a man of his own age.

Legends and Reality of Giotto's Youth, Down to the Revelation of the Assisi Frescoes (1267- 1300)

We know very little about Giotto's childhood and early training, not even whether "Giotto" was his original name or merely a diminutive of Biagio or Agnolo. The year of his birth is not recorded in any document but deduced from the fact that

the painter died in January 1337 at the age of seventy. However 1267 is a very likely date and follows closely after that of Dante in 1265.

Born into a peasant family at Colle di Vespignano, not far from Florence—where his father Bondone was "a worker of the earth, born illegitimate"—Giotto was described by early commentators (notably Lorenzo Ghiberti and then Vasari) as an infant prodigy. The encounter between the great master Cimabue and the shepherd boy scratching a drawing of sheep on a stone at Mugello, on the road to Bologna, is one of the most widely quoted examples of "natural talent" in the whole history of art. However implausible the ancient legend (though Luciano Bellosi has recently suggested it may be true), there was definitely a close relationship between Cimabue and Giotto, so that it is quite possible that they may have worked together on some paintings, such as the Madonna of the prepositorship at Castelfiorentino.

Cimabue's style marked the final development of Byzantine art in Italy: the poses of the figures, their gestures and lineaments, and his lack of interest in the representation of space all correspond to the rules dictated by Eastern tradition. But Cimabue also possessed a lofty and dramatic vision of sacred history, a sense of the conflict between good and evil which he translated into a new plastic energy in his paintings, with a powerful and expressive emotional impact.

The apprenticeship to Cimabue was followed by another equally important experience of Giotto's youth, a journey to Rome. Before he began work on the great new Basilica of San Francesco in Assisi, the young painter visited the "Eternal City" for the first time. There he found a city of thirty thousand inhabitants (half the population of Florence) with ancient monuments lying in ruin. Amidst the rubble of ancient Rome emerged the splendid early Christian basilicas, many of them decorated with mosaics and frescoes in the course of the thirteenth century. There was also an important school of Roman painting, led by artists such as Piero Cavallini, Jacopo Torriti and Filippo Rusuti. Without entirely abandoning Byzantine iconography, these Roman painters and mosaic-workers were recreating the serenity and monumentality of classical art: the papal city was giving birth once more to an imperial city, and one of the artists involved was Arnolfo di Cambio, who painted important ornamental cycles in Rome.

Though the earliest work confidently attributed to Giotto is the fresco cycle in Assisi (it has been suggested that there are traces of Giotto's youthful work among the mosaics in the Baptistry of Florence), critics agree on the decisive importance of the sojourn in Rome, so that it is debated whether Giotto came to Assisi in the train of Cimabue or as one of a group of artists coming from Rome. Be that as it may, the 1290s mark the beginning of his close relationship with the Franciscan order, which commissioned many of his later works.

The great architectural complex of the Convent and Basilica of San Francesco in Assisi began to be built only two years after the death of the saint in 1226; work went ahead rapidly, and it grew into the most important monument of Italian architecture and painting in the thirteenth and fourteenth centuries. An underground crypt (later walled up, then reopened in the eighteenth century) formed the lowest level and contains the tomb of Saint Francis. Above the crypt stands the large, shallow Lower Church, its architecture still Romanesque, completed shortly after 1230. Above it rises the Upper Church (Plate 1), consecrated in 1253. Like the church below, it has a broad nave without side aisles but is much taller, wholly Gothic in style. Great mullioned windows with stained glass make the interior bright, in contrast with the gloom and silence of the Lower Church, and the space is rhythmically divided into four simple crossvaulted bays. The great walls were left bare, ready to be decorated with frescoes.

Work went ahead simultaneously inside the two churches, but while the Lower Church, with its more highly articulated plan, provided a variety of chapels and other surfaces that could be entrusted to different artists, the great walls of the Upper Church suggested the need for a single coherent scheme of decoration, which is still visible despite the damage suffered by the frescoes over the centuries. The *Scenes from the Old and New Testaments* are linked to passages from the *Legenda Maior*, the story of the life and miracles of Saint Francis by Saint Bonaventura, written in 1260–1263. Saint Francis is presented historically, not in a hagiographical or anecdotal account; as if God's plan, through the precedents of the Bible and the Gospel, found a logical and direct consequence in the life of the saint.

In the years around 1277-1280 Cimabue made an outstanding contribution to the decoration of the left transept, including the vaulting, with frescoes that included the dramatic scene of the *Crucifixion*. Later, in around 1285, though Cimabue retained the supervision of the work, the execution of the frescoes passed to his collaborators, among whom Jacopo Torriti and Duccio da Boninsegna of Siena (then still a novice) were outstanding. Work thus began on the decoration of the upper parts of the nave, especially the spaces between the windows, with the *Scenes from the Old and New Testaments* set one above the other on two levels. It is in this phase that Giotto's hand first appears in the work, in the fourth bay. The attribution of certain scenes from the Old and New Testaments to Giotto is generally accepted, while the chronology is much harder to determine, c. 1290 being a probable date. In the vaulting of the entrance bay, better preserved than the side walls, there is a fresco of the *Four Church Fathers*, seated at desks and lecterns that simulate the mosaic-geometry typical of Romanesque work in Lazio, while small paintings of paired saints can be seen under the adjoining arch. Even more interesting are the few remaining parts of the Biblical and Gospel scenes between the windows. Divided into regular squares measuring three metres per side, these scenes are one of the most important sources for the study of Italian painting at the end of the thirteenth century. The personality of the youthful Giotto is at once evident, especially in the two *Scenes from the Life of Isaac* (Plates 2, 3) and the fragmentary *Entombment*, in the subtle attention paid to the interplay of expressions and feelings, while the narrative is based on deliberate, regular, classical rhythms, and not the urgently dramatic rhythms of Cimabue.

While Giotto collaborated with other important artists in *Scenes from the Old and New Testaments*, measuring himself against them, in the lower series he was working on his own. The lower part of the wall juts out slightly and seems to have been specially designed when the church was built to serve as a ground for a fresco cycle. The *Scenes from the Life of Saint Francis* (Plates

4–9), which start from the bottom of the right-hand wall then continue along the end wall onto the left-hand wall, mark the appearance of a new idea in art. Composed during the later 1290s, they tell the study of the life of Saint Francis from adolescence down to the miracles performed after his death. Without any iconographic precedents (save for the features of the saint), Giotto was free to handle the scenes as he chose. Only in some of the last scenes does a certain falling-off of the quality appear, a sign of the intervention of pupils. The novelty of these frescoes lies in the depiction of a flesh-and-blood Saint Francis (see the partial nude in the scene of *Saint Francis Renounces his Wordly Goods*, Plate 5), in the midst of his people (often represented as acting in unison, as in the *Death of the Knight of Celano*, Plate 9), in concrete, recognizable places (the square of Assisi forms the background to the *Saint Francis Honoured by a Simple Man of Assisi*, Plate 4); and above all in architectural or natural settings conceived in three-dimensional depth and closely related to the scene depicted. For example, the line of the hills in the *Saint Francis Giving His Cloak to a Poor Man* converges towards the saint's head, which thus becomes the vertex not just of the episode but of the whole landscape. Or in the *Miracle of the Crucifix* and the *Confirmation of the Rules*, the architectural settings are spatial "sets," depicted with an unprecedentedly three-dimensional vision, anticipating later studies of perspective. The iconostasis seen from behind in the *Christmas Crib at Greccio* (Plates 6, 7) is a notable example of this.

Without giving in to a purely biographical account, yet following the iconographical programme closely, Giotto produced a sequence of realistic images, figures and settings, breaking for good with the Byzantine style. The harmony of his scenes creates a moving and exciting narrative for the uninstructed faithful, while at the same time the frescoes are rich in interest and innovations for artists and men of culture.

Some episodes of the life of Saint Francis appear in a great panel painting with a gilt background, *Saint Francis Receiving the Stigmata* (Plate 10, signed by the artist) from the church of San Francesco in Pisa and now in the Louvre, dating from the same period as the frescoes at Assisi.

In 1300, when he had probably completed the

Scenes from the Life of Saint Francis, Giotto returned to Rome and was present at the Jubilee celebrations held by Pope Boniface VIII. In this period he painted a number of frescoes recorded in documents now mostly lost: there still exists a fragment of *Boniface VIII Proclaiming the Jubilee* in the church of San Giovanni in Laterano.

After Assisi and Rome, Giotto finally returned to Florence. Significant traces of his first period in Florence remain in the *Madonna* in San Giorgio della Costa, in some remnants of frescoes in the church of the Badia (which also possessed a polyptych, now in the Uffizi), and above all in the great *Crucifix* on a panel in the sacristy of Santa Maria Novella (Plate 11). This is the first version of a subject that Giotto repeated a number of times, and it shows his rejection of the elegant, rigid Byzantine style for a more direct anatomical representation. A significant detail is the use of a single nail securing both feet of Christ to the cross, which required the feet to be superimposed and foreshortened, instead of the highly simplified scheme of Byzantine tradition, in which each foot is pierced by a separate nail.

Giotto returned to Assisi even after his early period to supervise the decoration of the vaulting of the Lower Church (with *Franciscan Allegories*) and the *Magdalene Chapel*. In both cases the artist confined himself mainly to coordinating and supervising the work, leaving the execution of the frescoes to his pupils.

The Scrovegni Chapel and the Central Years of Giotto's Maturity (1300–1320)

Between 1304 and 1306 Giotto was working in Padua on the frescoes of the chapel erected by Enrico Scrovegni to expiate the sin of usury committed by his father, condemned by Dante in the *Inferno*. Though not mentioned in the records, it is highly likely that Giotto was responsible for the design of the building, which stands on the remains of the Roman amphitheatre in Padua, and so is also known as the Arena Chapel. The structure is simple, essential, and the interior is perfectly functional as a container for a complex fresco cycle: a single space, a nave without side-aisles, with narrow windows on one side only, the barrel-vaulting of the ceiling being painted as a starry sky with a number of divine figures (the *Madonna and Child*, the *Christ Blessing*, the *Evan-*

gelists, the *Four Church Fathers* within medallions). The iconographic scheme exalts the figure of the Madonna as the mother of Christ, who worked our Redemption, the means of salvation for mankind, who travel on their path between good and evil (represented in the fanciful *grisaille* allegorical figures decorating the base), towards the *Last Judgement*. This is the scene painted on the great end wall (Plate 13), organized around the figure of Christ, surrounded by ranks of angels dividing the blessed from the damned, who hurtle downwards amid the fearful torments of hell. The scene is crowded and full of life, but numerous details seem to have been entrusted to pupils. The same wall contains the portrait of Enrico Scrovegni dedicating the model of the chapel to the Madonna.

Along the sides and on the triumphal arch, ranged on three levels and forming a continuous sequence, run the *Stories from the Lives of Joachim and Anna* (Plates 16–19) and the *Scenes from the Life and Passion of Christ* (Plates 20–23; 25–27), for a total of thirty-six scenes. They are meant to be read in the same order as the *Scenes from the Life of Saint Francis* (Plates 4–9). Painted in a fairly brief period of time, the Paduan frescoes are the work in which Giotto first shows his mature powers, apparent in their great stylistic coherence, continuous formal mastery and their solemn affirmation of the dignity of the human figure and its central place in the episodes recounted.

Even more than at Assisi, Giotto dominated and organized the space in which his personages act. The figures are broad and compact, almost like geometrical solids, and they occupy physical volumes that are measurable in terms of dilated natural or architectural settings. The chronological order of the scenes begins with the vicissitudes of the parents of the Madonna. The scenes depicting the father of Maria an exile in the desert (for example *Joachim with the Shepherds*, Plate 15) are typical of the "psychological" arrangement of the elements of nature and the landscape, with solitary figures, as harsh and rugged as the hills in the background. The deep sentiments that form a bond between Joachim and Anna appear in the *Meeting at the Golden Gate* (Plates 18, 19) one of the fullest examples of Giotto's expressive powers, here embodied in the tender kiss exchanged by the two central figures.

With the *Nativity of the Virgin* (placed in the same architectural setting as the *Annunciation to Saint Anne*), also in the upper row of frescoes, we pass on to the left-hand wall. Of the various scenes into which the episode of the *Virgin's Wedding Feast* is divided, that of the *Watching of the Rods at the Altar* is highly moving and shows great energy in its composition: the group of priests and the suitors for the Virgin's hand form imposing masses. The figures of the *Archangel Gabriel* and the *Annunciation* on the triumphal arch link the left-hand wall with the right-hand one: they are set within identical architectural scenes, foreshortened, forming two full, sturdy masses, very different from the more sinewy outline of Giovanni Pisano's *Madonna and Child* placed on the altar together with other sculptures of two angels supporting candlesticks. In the centre of the triumphal arch there is the panel painting of God the Father, in a poor state of conservation.

The childhood of Christ, which begins with the *Visitation* in the triumphal arch, in the middle row of frescoes, opens with a number of episodes that are movingly intimate: the Madonna has her hair braided (a common hairstyle in the Veneto in the early fourteenth century). In the *Nativity* she is shown reclining, a pose unusual in painting but here very natural (Plate 20). In the *Flight into Egypt* (Plate 21), Giotto once again uses features of the landscape to intensify the psychological expressiveness of the figures. The Madonna and Child appear compact, clinging together, and set within the outline of a rock in the background. An inversion of this effect is seen in the *Baptism of Christ*, where the hillsides seem to open out symmetrically. This scene opens the sequence devoted to the miracles and Passion of Jesus. The *Betrayal of Judas* placed on the triumphal arch, links the two walls and indicates a shift to the lower series of frescoes. The features of the traitor are caricatured in those of the dark devil behind him.

The *Last Supper* (one of the episodes, together with the scene of the *Way to Calvary* and the *Ascension*, in which the hand of a collaborator is most evident), and the *Washing of the Feet* are placed within an identical pavilion, shown in perspective, which gives the scene an air of solemnity and deliberation, very different from the *Kiss of Judas* (Plates 22, 23), with the chaotic atmosphere surrounding the figure of Judas, petrified by the serene, severe gaze of Christ. The movement of the agitated crowd of figures derives from the dynamic composition, underscored by the waving of lanterns and pikes, here used with almost theatrical effect by Giotto. The central scenes on the wall (*Crucifixion*, *Lamentation over the Dead Christ*, Plates 25, 26; *Noli Me Tangere*, Plate 27), form almost a triptych; they are scenes often represented in art, and Giotto concentrates some of his most innovatory features in the treatment of space in these scenes. The grief of the angels around the Crucifixion is yet another demonstration of Giotto's sensitivity to human expression. The resurrected Christ, appearing to Mary Magdalene, moves lightly, elegantly, which has led to comparisons with the carvings of Pallas Athene by Phidias. In the scene of mourning in the *Lamentation*, the figures are set in a sequences of different visual planes that recede into the background, starting with the innovatory presence of the two figures seen from behind. Saint John, stooping over the body of Jesus, opens out his arms at right angles to the plane of the painting, making another breach in the two-dimensional space.

In the Scrovegni Chapel Giotto painted two *trompe l'œil* paintings. On the triumphal arch he simulated two chapels (Plate 28) that demonstrate his exceptional grasp of the rules of three-dimensional representation. A *Crucifix*, painted on panel, was also painted for the Scrovegni Chapel and is now in the Civic Museum in Padua (Plate 29): some scholars hold that it was painted by Giotto during a second sojourn in Padua in 1317, when he decorated the Palazzo della Ragione with frescoes that are now lost.

The period between the Scrovegni Chapel and the frescoes in the Bardi and Peruzzi Chapels in Santa Croce (in Florence), that is from about 1305 to 1320, is the "classical" phase of Giotto's work. During these years he still travelled widely, working in Rimini (where he produced the splendid *Crucifix* in the Tempio Malatestiano, Plate 31, regarded as his finest work in this genre) and Rome, where he returned in 1310 to execute the great mosaic with the *"Navicella" of Saint Peter* for the exterior of the Basilica Vaticana: nothing remains of this work save some heavily restored fragments.

His reputation and status grew steadily: financially and socially he was secure. He had married Ciuta (diminutive of "Ricevuta") di Lapo del Pela, by whom he had eight children, and he was able to make good use of his flair for business, investing his earnings as a painter in a series of successful deals. The paintings of this period are solemn, harmonious compositions, in which the figures are arranged regularly, without expressive excesses or unpleasing deformities. To this period belong works on a large scale, such as the *Ognissanti Altarpiece* in the Uffizi (Plate 30) and the later *Dormition of the Virgin* in the museum of Berlin. In the first room of the Uffizi, Giotto's *Madonna* is placed by two similar works by Cimabue and Duccio; the comparison shows that Giotto departed futher from the Byzantine schemes and much more emphatically, giving his figures solid, tangible volumes and setting them in a physical space. (The throne on which Giotto's *Madonna* is seated is a slender Gothic structure, very different from the massive Romanesque seats of the other two works.)

The Florentine Frescoes and the Last Phase: From Giotto to his Followers (1320–1337)

From 1320 on Giotto appears to have been particularly busy in Florence. Many of the works mentioned in the historical sources have been lost; others are scattered in different museums all over the world. This is the case with a great polyptych, consisting of five cusped panels and a predella with *Scenes from the Life and Passion of Christ*, laboriously reconstructed by scholars, starting from a *Saint Stephen* in the Horne Museum in Florence and the *Madonna with Child* in the National Gallery of Art in Washington, originally the centrepiece of the work. The small panels of the predella repeat subjects and compositions present in the Scrovegni Chapel. Between 1320 and 1325 Giotto worked assiduously in the chapels of the Florentine families that are to be found in the apse of the great church of Santa Croce, so confirming his close links with the Franciscan Order and also his position as the leading artist in Florence. The records tell us that he frescoed no fewer than four of the chapels; of these two remain, both belonging to banking families, on the right of the central apse. In both cases, the frescoes were completely repainted in the nineteenth century: the removal of the repaintings has only partially restored the scenes, but at least what we now have is his original work.

The Peruzzi Chapel, the first to be painted, contains *Scenes from the Lives of Saint John the Baptist and Saint John the Evangelist*, on the two side walls facing each other. Giotto's interest in perspective is even clearer here. He makes allowance for the point of view of the observer in this narrow, tall chapel. The architecture of the buildings in the paintings is very complex (as in *The Feast of Herod*), with interiors of different sizes and depths; even in the outdoor scenes (*Resuscitation of Drusiana*) the articulation of the urban and architectural spaces is unusually varied. The fresco of the *Vision of Saint John in Patmos* (Plate 36) is extremely powerful: it shows the saint sleeping and surrounded by the symbols of the Apocalypse appearing to him in a dream.

The adjacent Bardi Chapel repeats the theme, dear to Giotto, of the *Scenes from the Life of Saint Francis* (Plates 33-35), starting from the large fresco of *Saint Francis Receiving the Stigmata* on the entrance arch (Plate 35). Compared with the Assisi cycle, painted thirty years earlier, Giotto displays a firmer, more serene handling that extends more fully in space. Even the strongest feelings appear to be restrained by a sense of peace, which is also embodied in the broad, harmoniously distributed structures of the compositions. A good example is the *Examination of the Stigmata*, with the moving grief of the friars, mourning for the death of Saint Francis. The frescoes have suffered in the damage done to the chapel; the surviving parts, however, have a freshness of colour that is greater than the faded pictures in the Peruzzi Chapel.

In the Baroncelli Chapel, also in Santa Croce, there is the *Polyptych of the Coronation of the Virgin*, probably painted soon after the frescoes in the Bardi Chapel. Here there is extensive evidence of the work of pupils in the massed array of angels praising the Virgin and also in the massive figures in the central section. The individual collaborators who worked with Giotto in Assisi and Padua had by this time been replaced by a well-organized workshop, among whom certain relatives of Giotto and artists with a definite personality of their own were beginning to emerge. In

1327, together with Taddeo Gaddi and Bernardo Daddi, Giotto enrolled in the Guild of Physicians and Druggists, then opened to artists. A confirmation of the contribution of his assistants to the *Baroncelli Altarpiece* is given, paradoxically, by the fact that this work bears Giotto's signature, as if he were concerned to certify his supervision of the work. The Renaissance "reuse" of the polyptych, set within an elegant fifteenth century frame, is a point of added interest.

Between 1328 and 1333, after a decade spent working in Florence, Giotto set out on his travels again. He returned to Naples several times; there Robert of Anjou employed him on a number of works (including a series of frescoes in the Castel dell'Ovo), all now lost. In about 1330 he went to Bologna, where he coordinated the execution of the *Altarpiece in Bologna* (now in the Pinacoteca Nazionale, Plate 37), which he also signed conspicuously but was largely the work of pupils. Even more important was the *Stefaneschi Altarpiece* (Pinacoteca Vaticana, Rome; Plates 38, 39), dedicated to Saint Peter and commissioned by the cardinal Jacopo Caetani Stefaneschi for the high altar of the Basilica of Saint Peter. The polyptych, with its predella, was painted on both sides of the panel; on one side Christ in glory is flanked by depictions of the martyrdoms of Saint Peter and Saint Paul; on the other, Saint Peter is seated on his throne as the first pope amidst other saints. The donor (as in the case of Enrico Scrovegni) is shown in the act of donating the polyptych. Though it shows numerous signs of the work of an assistant (possibly from Siena), much of the work is of high quality, directly from Giotto's own hand, while the figure of the kneeling donor shows his insight as a portraitist.

The Bologna and Rome polyptyches are among the last works by Giotto to come down to us. On 12 April 1334, the artist was appointed the "*magister et gubernator*" of the Opera di Santa Reparata, i.e. overseer of the construction of Florence cathedral. His architectural ability was clearly shown in the foundation and the first storey of the bell tower, of which the elevation was wholly completed during the second half of the fourteenth century.

Between 1335 and 1336 Giotto, accompanied by his pupils, moved to the court of Azzone Visconti in Milan. As at Naples, there is now no trace of his work in Milan, save in panels and frescoes by his followers.

Giotto then returned to Florence to supervise work on the bell tower. He died in his seventies on 8 January 1337, and was buried in the cathedral with great public honours.

The Legacy

According to a well-known aphorism of Roberto Longhi, the only true "Giottesque" artist is Giotto himself. He alone, in fact, had the energy to radically renew the Italian artistic tradition. His followers, even the great artists, failed to equal their master. Giotto's frequent travels fostered the birth of schools of followers all over Italy.

A typical example is the school of Rimini, perhaps the first to embrace the master's innovations and translate them into a pleasing narrative technique. The use of perspective and geometrical organization was to take root most strongly, however, in Florence, which took the place of Assisi as the avant-garde of artistic development during the fourteenth century. In the same places as Giotto had once worked, starting from the church of Santa Croce, masters such as Maso di Banco, Agnolo Gaddi, Bernardo Daddi and the relatives of Giotto Stefano and Giottino formed a compact group, inspired by a solid sense of realism. But Dante's prophecy that Giotto would be followed by a successor capable of surpassing him, just as Giotto had surpassed Cimabue, seems to have been mistaken.

As Millard Meiss has amply demonstrated, the "Black Death" of 1348 led to a far-reaching revision of attitudes in Tuscan culture and art. Painting returned to a vision of man's destiny as depending on the will of God, which Giotto's paintings had to some extent limited. So for about half a century there was a return to a severely hieratic art. Giotto was admired and studied, but more for his craftsmanship than his composition. The *novelle* of Boccaccio and Sacchetti recall the historical figure of the master, as ugly as he was shrewd; there emerges from their writings a nostalgia for a kind of art that no one was now capable of practising. The *Libro dell'Arte* written at the end of the fourteenth century by Cennino Cennini is a compendium of Giotto's technique, minutely descriptive of every phase of preparation and execution of the work of art.

At the start of the fifteenth century Giotto's example became the essential basis for humanism. Masaccio was hailed as "Giotto reborn" for his application of the rules of perspective to the painting of both figures and architecture. At a time when the rich and ornate late-Gothic school was dominant, Giotto's strong, plain style returned to favour with the linearity of Brunnelleschi's architecture (who raised the dome of the cathedral alongside Giotto's bell tower) and the plastic energy of Donatello's sculptures. The revival of Giotto, seen as the forerunner of the Florentine Renaissance, was ratified by a public decree to raise a monument to him, with a sculpture by Benedetto da Maiano and an inscription by Politian. In the same period the young Michelangelo was practising by copying Giotto's frescoes, deriving from them his taste for figures that occupied a robust volume.

From the Cinquecento on, despite the high praise bestowed by Vasari and all subsequent art historians, Giotto's reputation and that of all the "primitives" tended to suffer an eclipse. The painters from before the mid-fifteenth century were regarded as mere "curiosities" by the learned, and many of their works were irremediably destroyed or damaged. The Bardi and Peruzzi Chapels, for example, were whitewashed.

In the course of the nineteenth century, in the wake of the recovery begun by the German Romantics, Giotto was given increasing attention, and his works were rediscovered and sometimes restored injudiciously. Towards the end of the century the frescoes in Assisi were being studied in depth: the work of Rintelen (*Giotto und die Giotto-Apokriphen*, published in 1912) began the long polemic over attributions, summed up in 1939 by Offner with a long article with the significant title of *Giotto-non Giotto*. While the critics were divided, Giotto was also an important model for painters: Cézanne and the Cubists regarded him as an important point of reference, and Carlo Carrà (who also devoted a monograph to Giotto) made him the basis of the Italian school known as the Novecento. The critical research of the postwar period, with restoration work and further discoveries, has covered a wide range of topics, with particular attention to Giotto's representation of space, the chronology of his works, and his early training.

Anthology of Comments

Cimabue believed he held sway/ In the field of painting,/But now Giotto is all the cry/ So that the other's fame is eclipsed.
(Dante, *Purgatorio*, Canto XI, c. 1310)

Giotto possessed an intellect of such excellence that nothing of nature, the mother of all things and responsible for the continual turning of the heavens, did he fail to paint with stylus and pencil and brush similar to the original... so that often the things he painted led men's eyes to fall into error, believing them real. For this reason, having restored art to the light, which for many centuries had been buried under the errors of those that sought to delight the ignorant rather than please the intellect of the wise, he can truly be called one of the leading lights of the glory of Florence; and all the more so, since with great humility he, a master of others in his art, always refused to let others call him *maestro*; which title, rejected by him, shone all the more brightly in him, in proportion as it was avidly usurped by those that knew less than he or by his pupils.
(G. Boccaccio, *Decamerone*, VI Day, V Novella, c. 1350)

He translated the art of painting from Greek into Latin and made it modern; and he possessed the most accomplished art that anyone has ever had.
(C. Cennini, *Il Libro dell'Arte*, c. 1390)

Among the other questions raised, one, whose name was Orcagna, the master builder of the noble oratory of Nostra Donna d'Orto San Michele (the church of Orsanmichele in Florence), asked: "Who was the greatest master of painting, apart from Giotto, down to the present day?" Some said Cimabue, others Stefano, others Bernardo [Daddi] and still others Buffalmacco, and some said one, some said another. Taddeo Gaddi, who was of the company, said: "Certainly there have been very fine painters, who painted in such a way that human nature is unable to do better. But that art is gradually disappearing day by day."
(F. Sacchetti, *Novelle*, CXXXVI, c. 1395)

The art of painting began to rise in Etruria, in a place near the city of Florence that is called Ves-

pignano. A boy was born of wonderful intellect, who happened to be drawing a sheep when Cimabue the painter passed by that way along the road to Bologna, and saw the boy sitting on the ground and drawing a sheep on a piece of stone. He was filled with admiration for the lad, who though young was drawing so well. Seeing that he was naturally gifted as an artist, he asked the lad what his name was. "My name is Giotto and my father's is Bondone and he lives in this house near at hand," the boy said. Cimabue went with Giotto to his father (he made a very fine appearance), and asked the father to entrust him with the boy. The father was very poor. He allowed the boy to go with Cimabue, and so Giotto became his pupil.
(L. Ghiberti, *Commentarii*, II, c. 1450)

He went to Assisi, a city of Umbria, being summoned there by Fra Giovanni di Muro della Marca, then the general of the friars of Saint Francis. There, in the upper church, he painted frescoes under the strip traversing the windows on the two sides of the church, with thirty-two stories of the life and works of Saint Francis, sixteen on either side, so perfectly painted that he won great fame. And truly there can be seen in this work a great variety not just in the gestures and attitudes of the different figures, but also in the composition of all the stories. It is also wonderful to see the diversity of the garments of those times and certain imitations and observations of the natural world.
(G. Vasari, *Le Vite dei più eccellenti pittori, scultori et architettori*, 1568)

He was also a sculptor and his models were preserved down to the age of Lorenzo Ghiberti. Nor did he lack good examples. There were ancient marbles in Florence, which can now be seen at the cathedral (without mentioning what he later saw in Rome), and their merit, already acknowledged by Niccola and Giovanni Pisani, could hardly have been ignored by Giotto, whom nature had endowed with a sensibility for the true and the beautiful. When one looks at certain of his male heads, certain squared forms, so remote from the slender forms of his contemporaries, or his feeling for rare, natural, majestic draperies, and certain poses of his figures, which

have an air of decorum and restraint, then it is very hard to believe that he did not learn a great deal from ancient marbles.
(L. Lanzi, *Storia pittorica dell'Italia*, 1795–1796)

Giotto changed the method of preparing colours hitherto in use and changed the concept and direction of pictorial representation. He kept to the present and to reality; and his figures and effects were used to represent the life around him. Together with these tendencies, there was also the fortunate circumstance that not only did costume become freer and life gayer in Giotto's time, but the cult of new saints also came about then, saints that had flourished in times not long before the painter's own lifetime. In the content of his paintings, the naturalness of the bodily figures themselves was thus implicit, as well as the presentation of definite characters, actions, situations, attitudes and movements. Because of this tendency, there was a gradual (though relative) loss of that grandiose, sacred austerity that was the foundation of the previous school of art. Wordly attitudes took root and spread, and in keeping with the spirit of the time, Giotto, too, accepted burlesque alongside pathos.
(G.F. Hegel, *Vorlesung über Aesthetik*, 1829)

With the achievements of Giotto and Duccio began the eclipse of the mediaeval figurative vision. For the depiction of a closed, interior space conceived as a concave body signifies more than a simple consolidation of objects; it entails an authentic revolution in the formal valuation of the painted surface: it is no longer the wall or panel on which the forms of individual things or figures are laid, but it has once more become the transparent plane through which we may believe we are looking at an open space, though circumscribed in all directions: a "figurative plane" in the fullest sense of the word.
(E. Panofsky, *La prospettiva come "forma simbolica,"* 1927)

Under the burden of my years I traverse the field from which emerge the walls of the ancient arena, like the bones of a skeleton picked clean; but when I cross the threshold of the Scrovegni Chapel, time suddenly winds backward and I am a child again, in my playroom. Toys to right and left of me. A double row of toys, in the midst of which the man, now a child again, passes solemn and lightly, in the always-young light of earthly immortality. Giotto's painting is the mother of toys. This is his supreme quality, his secret quality. The composition follows the instructions for "Little Architects." These pure, vivid colours are like those that shone on the balls and ninepins and dice of my childhood. And there I can see my rocking horse. Art always rekindles the lights of the lost paradise, which the gloomy hands of non-artists return always to extinguish. But Giotto revives not just the image of that lost paradise, but also the games that took place in that light that was soft to the touch, in that life that seemed to be enclosed in pearl, the games we played to pass the timeless time. Here, as in the art of ancient Greece, nothing is stronger than the strength of men, everything is made to be dismantled and then assembled differently, everything is portable. Nothing has yet been darkened by the shadow of sin. No cloud has yet formed in that clear sky. Silver nails secure this unchanging serenity, this intense boundless turquoise.

(A. Savinio, *Ascolto il tuo cuore, città*, 1944)

No scientific treatise can describe human events of the earth and the heart with such great immediacy and effectiveness as does painting, through the use of form, which is incarnation and purification, through style, which is the enduring shape of passions suffered and dominated. This was how Giotto *saw* and felt the value of the human figure first: he possessed a feeling for large, imposing composition, a sense of the weight and volume of things, and to his language submits the exquisite colour that enlivens unpredictably changing surface, which a wholly Tuscan sense of form has drawn and caught with precision. A quality that until the coming of Michelangelo remained intact even when confronted by the allurements of Leonardo's softer colours. He understood space, atmosphere, different planes, he was the first person to have a feeling for the external world, meaning landscapes, mountains, trees and rocks, whose austerity and heroism, like his human figures, bear the singular and unifying touch of a cosmic vision.

(G. Delogu, *Antologia della pittura italiana*, 1947)

If one stands at the centre of the paving of the Scrovegni Chapel, in the spot best suited to take in at a single glance the wall in which the apse is set, it at once becomes plain... that the two *trompe-l'oeil* apertures have the effect of "opening up" the wall, with the aim of affecting the architecture of the votive chapel. The convincing illusion thus created is underscored by the two Gothic vaults running towards a single centre which lies on the axis of the church, that is in the real, existential depth of the apse. The internal light starts from the centre and spreads through the two bays, even onto the columns and jambs of the apertures of the windows not with "abstract" ultramarine but a pale azure colour, which combines with the real blue outside the windows in the apse: so real is the illusion that one feels an impulse to wait and see the swallows swooping down from the nearby eaves of the church of the Eremitani.

(R. Longhi, "Giotto spazioso," in *Paragone*, 31, 1952)

Between 1260 and 1290 Cimabue, who worked in Rome and Florence, was undoubtedly an Italian—and even European—painter of outstanding greatness and poetical energy; and he was also the painter possessed of the highest and most complex culture in the great mediaeval tradition. In him we find a moral force, an evocative and expressive power, that can still be felt pressing against the mediaeval forms and transforming them until they became something new, but always within limits that he seems to have suffered from dramatically, seeking to overcome them, yet that still hemmed him in. And in this clash that strength swelled and was exalted, displaying itself in dilated, superhuman forms.

Giotto inherited the poetic message of Cimabue, but at once added the awareness that mankind now had other means to express their truth, in all its fullness and variety and not merely in that vertical ascent or unmeasurably profound sense of drama. With Giotto a new cycle opened in serenity. Cimabue was heroic passion dilating and overwhelming humanity. Giotto was harmony and measure dominating and containing the passsions, the greatness of man.

(G. Gnudi, under the entry "Giotto," in the *Enciclopedia Universale dell'Arte*, VI, 1958)

18

In the commentary on the *Commedia* by an anonymous Florentine we find it said that the painter, having become a master builder in his old age, "composed and designed the marble bell tower of Santa Reparata in Florence: a noteworthy bell tower and very costly. He committed two errors: the first that it had no foundations, the second that it was too narrow. These things struck his heart with such sorrow that he fell ill and died." The "errors" were merely the gossip of backbiters, for the bell tower showed clearly that the foundations were strong and the marble shaft was, in fact, of the right proportions. But the pupil of Arnolfo, the artist who had painted so many bold, elaborate works of achitecture, may actually have died, on 8 January 1337, when the bell tower was only a few yards high, nursing the doubt that he had erred in his only real work of architecture.

(P. Bargellini, *Belvedere. L'Arte Gotica*, 1961)

The Scrovegni Chapel was built in the place of a more modest and ancient structure, before which a sacred play was represented every year on the theme of the Annunciation and the other Stories of Maria.

There was nothing more natural than that Giotto, so observant of whatever went on about him, should have watched the sacred play of Padua while preparing to paint those same scenes on the walls of the chapel then being built..., and recalled the emotions and the narrative clarity in the arrangement of the various phases of the performance, together with the evocative value of certain architectural backdrops. So that he left on the chapel walls a more enduring spectacle, which was the official recognition, the seal and lasting record of the sacred play... It is impossible to ignore the possibility that alongside Giotto the architect there also exists what, in modern terms, might be described as a Giotto the "set-designer"—Giotto as the supreme director of gestures and feelings adapted to the actors in an episode, stage-managing his creations, those simple yet very modern actors that he set out in his magical "living picture," asking of each one of them, and hence of himself, the greatest intensity of expression with the greatest economy of means.

(M. Bacci, *Giotto*, 1966)

On the threshold of the year 2000, which may well loom up with greater terrors than the first millennium, this exploration of the ethical and poetical unity of the whole Middle Ages—and with the highly tangible example of Giotto, from the lyrical Giotto of Assisi to the tragic artist of Padua—is a profound lesson, and may even be a summons to salvation. Our age, and even more the millenium about to be born out of the current throes of the planet, seems to promise to be more mediaeval than classical or Renaissance... Even the modern age... has already created more than one "summa," perhaps desecrated but restorative. But until the recent past we were barely capable of a merely unambiguous and unilateral "summa," which aimed at isolated values but perhaps tomorrow like Giotto—we will be willing to create a "summa" that is once more unified yet many-sided.

(G. Vigorelli, "Giotto e l'invito all'unità," in *L'opera completa di Giotto*, edited by E. Bacceschi, 1967)

In presenting the faithful with the life of Saint Francis (in the Assisi frescoes), Giotto is now tender, now solemn, now dramatic, now serene, now familiar, now lyrical, now mystical, now popular, now apostolical, now a chronicler. He alternates observation of the contemporary world with the admonishment of the eternal, the miraculous with the everyday. Intended as hagiography, this fresco cycle seems to have been inspired by a natural heroism, a familiar sense of the supernatural, unattainable yet accessible (isn't all great poetry like this?). The saint is the hero of the human: not a model, but an example, and in the infinite distance that separates us from sanctity we yet share in his life. In this sense the stories of Saint Francis in Assisi are one of the least clerical monuments of all religious art.

(G. Pampaloni, *Giotto ad Assisi*, 1981)

What is more modern in all Western art in around 1290–1295 than these stories of Saint Francis? And not just in the reappropriation of the visible world in terms of spaces and volumes: this feature of his work, which after almost a thousand years meant once more seeing a value in the world of phenomena that man can verify through his own experience (as opposed to the so-called realism of the Middle Ages, which conceived the physical world as a symbol of the "true" reality, that of the next world), was part of a much wider reconsideration of the world and man in more natural and earthly terms. All those conventional graphic deformations of Byzantine origin disappeared from the human figure, whereas Cimabue and the young Duccio had only softened them... The human anatomy grew normal again, acquiring a degree of truth never achieved before.

A quite good example is the partial nude in *Saint Francis Renounces his Worldly Goods*, which—despite its chrysalid-like awkwardness that was typical of nudes all through the fourteenth century, reveals a remarkable degree of truthfulness in the depiction of the shoulder blades and ribs which must have amazed his contemporaries. The profiles of his faces re-acquire that positive value that had been obstinately denied for almost a thousand years, or at least the neutrality and normality typical of everyday experience. For the first time figures were again shown smiling in a painting.

(L. Bellosi, *La pecora di Giotto*, 1985)

The first to be amazed by Giotto's great talents not just as an artist, but also as an entrepreneur and a man who made his own fortune, were his contemporaries. Giotto's legend spread rapidly because his artistic career developed at a wholly unprecedented speed, with exceptional powers of innovation and also thanks to the fact that the new and modern features of his work were so outstanding. And it is also clear that Giotto's works made the old methods followed by his predecessors look old-fashioned, both because of the way he organized his workshop and also because of the great refinement of his aesthetic achievement.

(S. Bandera Bistoletti, *Giotto. Catalogo completo*, 1989)

1

1. Upper Church, Assisi, interior. The bright interior, one of the prototypes of Italian Gothic, was planned with a view to its decoration with a complex series of frescoes. Work began on them in 1280, and they were distributed in all the available spaces. The iconographic scheme required a close symbolical relationship between the Scenes from the New and Old Testaments (Plates 2,3), painted in the upper sections of the nave and along the transept, while the Scenes from the Life of Saint Francis (Plates 4–9) are ranged along the plinth and meant to be read as the exemplary fulfilment of the teaching of the Bible. The decoration began in the transept and continued along the sides in the upper section. After the first scenes had been painted by unknown artists, Cimabue was made responsible for the work, aided by collaborators and a group of painters from Rome. Giotto gradually made his first contributions in the last decade of the thirteenth century, painting one of the vaults and some of the Biblical scenes (which have deteriorated badly) level with the windows. Later he became the leading figure in the work, and began the decoration of the lower part of the wall with the Scenes from the Life of Saint Francis.

By the time he was thirty Giotto was able to display his own highly personal style, not just in the articulation of the separate scenes, but also in the narrative coherence of the whole cycle. Many years later Giotto returned to Assisi to supervise work on fresco cycles in the Lower Church.

2

2, 3. Isaac Rejects Esau, *c. 1290,*
fresco. Upper Church, Assisi.
The attribution of this fresco to Giotto
is supported by many critics. It belongs
to the Scenes from the Old and
New Testaments, *frescoed in the*
strip between the windows, initially
under the supervision of the Roman

artists Filippo Rusuti and Jacopo
Torriti. Despite the precarious state
of conservation of this work, the young
Giotto here gives us a precocious
sample of spatial coherence and a
sensitive rendering of the expressions
of the figures, throwing off the rigid
conventions of Byzantine tradition.

4

4. Saint Francis Honoured
by Simple Man of Assisi, *1295–
1300, fresco. Upper Church, Assisi.
One of the moments in Saint Francis'
youth, with an urban setting based
on reality.
A man is laying his mantle before*

*Saint Francis in the central square
of Assisi, with the classical elevation
of the Roman temple dedicated to
Minerva and the Palazzo Comunale.
Identification of the buildings is
facilitated by the fair state of
preservation of the fresco.*

5

5. Saint Francis Renounces his Worldly Goods, *1295–1300, fresco. Upper Church, Assisi.*
Saint Francis's decisive rejection of his father and his wealth is underscored by means of a sharp break in the composition. The saint, half-naked and clad in the cloak of the bishop of Foligno, looks up at a hand emerging from the sky, while the people of Assisi cluster around his father and restrain him. Two complicated buildings, naively foreshortened but drawn with a highly developed feeling for volume, stress the division of the action into two blocks.

6

6, 7. The Christmas Crib
at Greccio, *1295–1300, fresco.
Upper Church, Assisi.
The scene is clearly related to that
of the* Nativity *in the* Scenes from
the Old and New Testaments

*(Plates 2, 3), frescoed in the upper
section of the nave and forming a
"precedent" for episodes from the life
of Saint Francis.
Giotto's ability to measure space in
depth here creates a scene*

*of great intensity, with the iconostasis
seen from behind, hence with the
Crucifix shown in outline, as are the
other objects that project toward the
background of the fresco, crowded
with the faithful.*

7

8

8. Saint Francis Preaching before Pope Honorius III, *1295–1300, fresco. Upper Church, Assisi. Giotto's study of space gradually develops in awareness. The three-dimensional "box" of the chamber in which the debate takes place is stressed by the skilful arrangement of the architecture and the human figures, who serve as a yardstick for the volumes. Like all the scenes from this cycle, this one has suffered from heavy restoration.*

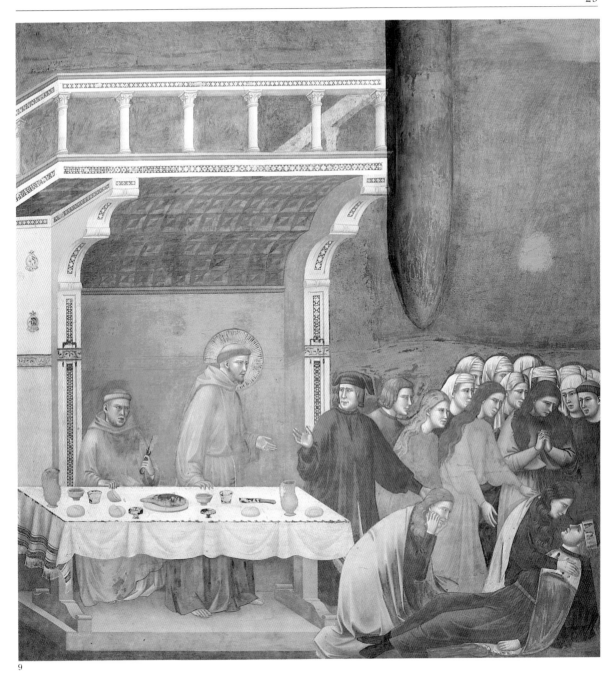

9

9. The Death of the Knight
of Celano, *1295–1300, fresco.
Upper Church, Assisi.*
*The subject records the instantaneous
realization of a prophecy of Saint
Francis, that the Knight of Celano
would receive eternal salvation but
also that his death would be*

*immediate. The opposition of the voids
and solids in the composition link the
figures with the setting. The figure of
the saint acts as a link between the two
spaces. In the mourners around the
body of the Cavaliere, Giotto expresses
a choral drama, with a wide range of
feelings and expressions.*

10. Saint Francis Receiving the Stigmata, *c. 1300, panel, 314 x 162 cm. Louvre, Paris. This well-preserved work comes from the church of San Francesco in Pisa, so confirming the close link between Giotto and the Franciscan Order throughout his career. The use of the traditional gilt background limits the effect of depth obtained in the Assisi frescoes but it endows the scenes— especially the three small images at the bottom—with a delicate poetry.*

11. The Crucifix, *c. 1300, panel, 578 x 406 cm. Sacristy of Santa Maria Novella, Florence. This is the earliest of Giotto's shaped panel paintings of the Crucifix. The divergence of Giotto's approach from the Byzantine scheme is already notable. This appears in the naturalness of the pose, the delicate lineaments, the simplicity of the loin cloth and the superimposition of the feet, pierced by a single nail.*

11

12

12. Scrovegni Chapel, *Padua,*
view of the interior toward the rear
wall.
Commissioned by Enrico Scrovegni in
atonement of the sin of usury
committed by his father, the chapel is
simply planned, perhaps inspired by
Giotto himself, with tall single light
windows running down one side only.
The intense blue of the sky appears in
many scenes, linking them with the
ceiling, underscoring the poignant
coherence of the underlying concept.

In the lower section, on a plinth
painted to imitate marble, runs a
series of grisaille *allegorical figures*
of the vices and virtues. Along the
walls and the triumphal arch that
closes the little choir of the chapel,
there are three superimposed orders
of Scenes from the Life of
Joachim and Anna, *and* Scenes
from the Lives of the Virgin and
Christ. *On the ceiling there are*
medallions with the Evangelists *and*
the Four Church Fathers. *The*

iconographic scheme is based on the
redemption of man through the life of
Jesus, and is completed by the Last
Judgement *on the end wall.*
The fair state of conservation does
justice to the numerous innovations
made by Giotto in the use of perspective
and the depiction of feeling.

13. Enrico Scrovegni Dedicating the
Chapel to the Madonna, *detail of the*
Last Judgement, *1304–1306, fresco.*
Scrovegni Chapel, Padua.

15

14. Inconstancy, *1304–1306, fresco.
Scrovegni Chapel, Padua.
This is one of the emblems of the vices
and virtues that run along the
opposite sides of the plinth. Giotto uses
a* grisaille *technique to suggest bas-
reliefs. They comprise a very vivid
series of symbolic figures, freed from
the traditional canons of art and
based on visual impact.*

15. Joachim with the Shepherds
*1304–1306, fresco. Scrovegni
Chapel, Padua.
The sequence of the scenes begins from
the end of the chapel at the top of the
left-hand wall, with the stories of the
parents of the Virgin. Giotto uses the
landscape to intensify the
psychological effect of the situations of
the characters. In this case the rugged
background stresses the solitude of the
sturdy masses of the three figures.*

16

16, 17. Joachin's Dream,
1304–1306, fresco. Scrovegni
Chapel, Padua.
The identification of the human figure
with a regular geometrical form is
significantly confirmed here by the
"cubic" shape of the sleeping Joachim.
The silence of the scene is broken by
the flock of sheep. Giotto here returns
to a naturalistic subject reminiscent
of his legendary meeting with
Cimabue when he was a boy.

18

18, 19. Meeting at the Golden
Gate, 1304–1306, fresco. Scrovegni
Chapel, Padua.
Joachim is greeted on his return by
Anna's affectionate embrace. This is
one of the most celebrated scenes in the
whole cycle. Here Giotto takes
advantage of the dramatic situation to
represent human expressions that had
been absent from art for almost a
thousand years: a smile, a kiss,
personal emotion.

20

20. The Nativity, *1304–1306,*
fresco. Scrovegni Chapel, Padua.
This belongs to the stories of the
childhood of Christ, which begin on
the right-hand side. Starting with the
middle series, the tone of the frescoes
grows more familiar. The departures
from the conventions of the past
are increasingly frequent, adding
to the sense of spontaneity in the
narrative. Note the reclining position
of Mary, who places Jesus in the
manger with an expression of deep
tenderness.

21

21. Flight into Egypt, *1304–1306,*
fresco. Scrovegni Chapel, Padua.
The landscape is again used to
intensify the effect of the whole and
give a structure to the composition:
the hillsides follow the rhythm of the
action, isolating the figures.

22

22, 23. The Kiss of Judas,
*1304–1306, fresco. Scrovegni
Chapel, Padua.*
*This scene is one of the most animated
and crowded, though it centers on the
motionless heads of Judas and Christ.
The gesture of betrayal can be*
*compared with the embrace of Joachim
and Anna, on the same wall. Giotto,
who is normally more restrained and
deliberate, here confers a dynamism on
the nocturnal scene of the betrayal,
heightened by the pikes, torches and
lanterns waving in the air.*

25

24. Jonah Swallowed by the
Whade, *1304–1306, fresco.*
Scrovegni Chapel, Padua.
Along the left-hand walls of the chapel
there are no windows and Giotto used
the space available to insert broad
decorative bands, with small biblical
scenes meant to prefigure events in the
Gospels. The prophet swallowed by the
whale and emerging after three days
in its belly is painted between the
scenes of the Crucifixion *and the*
Lamentation *(Plates 25, 26) to*
foreshadow symbolically and
iconographically the death of Christ
and His resurrection after three days.

25, 26. The Lamentation
over the Dead Christ, *1304–1306,*
fresco. Scrovegni Chapel, Padua.
This scene epitomizes many of Giotto's
innovations at Padua: the use of the
landscape as an important element
in the composition and not as a mere
neutral backdrop; his concern for
human feelings; the sophistication
of the narrative scheme, with figures
seen from behind and the variety of

despairing gestures among the angels.
The way the different elements are
arranged in depth has reached a high
degree of development here: the two
Marys are seen from behind, then
there is the body of Christ, then the
Madonna, with three different planes
ranged toward the back of the scene.
Saint John, with his arms outstretched
at right angles to the plane of the picture
further dilates the pictorial space.

27

27. Noli Me Tangere, *1304–1306,*
fresco. Scrovegni Chapel, Padua.
The elegant "cross-step" taken by
Christ as he moves away from Mary
Magdalene is combined with the inert
sleep of the soldiers by the empty
sepulchre. The theme of "Noli Me
Tangere" is thus united with that
of the Resurrection.

28

28. "Coretto" or Votive Chapel,
1304–1306, frescos. Scrovegni
Chapel, Padua.
On the triumphal arch of the chapel,
on the bottom level, Giotto has
imitated two little cross-vaulted
chapels with Gothic windows. This
was the first example of "pure"
perspective, without figures, simply to
create the illusion of space opening
out beyond the surface of the painting.

29. Crucifix, 1304–1306/1317?,
panel, 223 x 164 cm.
Musei Civici, Padua.
The shaped panel of medium
dimensions and in a fair state of
preservation comes from the Scrovegni
Chapel. It is not clear if it is of the
same period as the frescoes or was
painted in a second sojourn in Padua
in 1317.

30. Enthroned Madonna
(Ognissanti Altarpiece),
1306–1310, panel , 325 x 204 cm.
Uffizi, Florence.
This composition, in a good state of
conservation and recently restored,
belongs to the Tuscan tradition of the
Madonna with a gilt background on
a pentagonal panel. The solid volumes
of Giotto's figures, deliberately related
to geometrical solids, stand out within
a throne of Gothic architecture,
slender and elegant. The gesture
of the two kneeling angels, supporting
vases of flowers, is unusual.

29

32

32. Saint Stephen, *1320–1325,*
panel, 84 x 54 cm. Museo Horne,
Florence.
This panel is in excellent condition.
It was originally part of a polyptych,
now divided up among various
museums. The central panel is
of the Madonna, *and is now in the*
National Gallery of Art in
Washington. This Saint Stephen *is*
one of Giotto's works which shows most
care for the transparency of the
colours, laid on with rare delicacy.

31. Crucifix, *c. 1310, panel,*
430 x 303 cm. Tempio Malatestiano,
Rimini.
Evidence of a period spent in Rimini
(in c. 1310) and a landmark in the
development of painting in the area,
this is the finest example of this
particular genre. The careful, delicate

study of anatomy is favoured by a
sensitive use of light, which glances
off the elongated limbs. Christ is
shown as already dead, and his
features do not show the grimace
typical of earlier tradition. The plate
is in good condition, though the small
figures at the ends have been removed.

33

33, 34. Saint Francis Renounces
his Worldly Goods, *fresco, c. 1325.*
Santa Croce, Bardi Chapel, Florence.
Giotto's most intense activity in
Florence was concentrated on the
church of Santa Croce. The records
tell us that no fewer than four chapels
were decorated with frescoes by him.
After the destruction of some and the
repainting of others (partly because

they were regarded as "primitive"
works in the eighteenth and nineteenth
centuries) the cycles in the two chapels
of the bankers Peruzzi and Bardi, to
the right of the great chapel, alone
survive. They were painted after
1320. Convered with whitewash in the
past, they are in poor condition but
they reveal the direction of Giotto's
development after he left Padua.

He enriched the expressive and
dynamic resources of his work,
without losing any of the dignity
of the volumes of the human figures
and architectural elements.
The Bardi Chapel, which was
dedicated to Saint Francis, enables us
to compare the treatment of certain
scenes with the cycle in Assisi
of thirty years earlier.

35

35. Saint Francis Receiving the Stigmata, *c. 1325, fresco. Santa Croce, Bardi Chapel, Florence. Painted on the arch of the entrance to the Bardi Chapel, the fresco testifies to Giotto's achievements in the representation of the human body. Compared with his work in Padua,* *where the figures were composed as regular geometrical shapes, this Saint Francis has a complex volume, achieved through the combination of various solid figures. As in the Peruzzi Chapel, Giotto allows for the position of the viewer below the picture.*

36

36. Vision of Saint John
in Patmos, *c. 1325, fresco. Santa
Croce, Peruzzi Chapel, Florence.
The Peruzzi Chapel is dedicated to
Saint John the Evangelist and Saint
John the Baptist. The frescoes have
faded somewhat. They possess great
dramatic intensity. This lunette shows
Saint John with the jagged outline
of the island of Patmos, during his
vision of the Apocalypse, whose
symbols appear in the semicircle in
the sky.*

37

*37. Altarpiece in Bologna, c. 1330,
panels, 91 x 340 cm. Pinacoteca
Nazionale, Bologna.
An important example of Giotto's late
work and his relationship with his
well-organized workshop. The
polyptych is important in the
development of the Bologna school
of painting in the fourteenth century.
The structure of the whole is
overshadowed by the prominence of the
individual, solid figures of the saints
and the Madonna.*

38

38, 39. Stefaneschi Altarpiece,
c. 1330, panel, 220 x 245 cm.
Pinacoteca Vaticana, Rome.
Intended for the high altar of the
Basilica of San Pietro, this is the best
preserved of all Giotto's paintings
executed for Rome. The client who
commissioned it was the cardinal
Jacopo Caetani Stefaneschi, who is
portrayed on the altarpiece, which is
painted on both sides. The cardinal's
gesture is curious: he is holding a
representation of the polyptych in
which a diminutive image of the
cardinal appears holding the
painting.

Essential Bibliography

M. Bacci, *Giotto*, Florence 1966.

L'opera completa di Giotto, edited by E. Baccheschi, Milan 1967.

F. Bologna, *Novità su Giotto. Giotto al tempo della cappella Peruzzi*, Turin 1969.

Giotto e il suo tempo, papers from the conference for the eighth centenary of Giotto's birth (Rome 1967), Rome 1971.

G. Previtali, *Giotto e la sua bottega*, 2nd ed., Milan 1974.

Da Giotto al Mantegna, exhibition catalogue edited by L. Grossato, Palazzo della Ragione, Padua 1974.

L. Bellosi, *Giotto*, Florence 1981.

C. Brandi, *Giotto*, Milan 1983.

L. Bellosi, *La pecora di Giotto*, Turin 1985.

G. Bonsanti, *Giotto*, Padua 1985.

S. Bandera Bistoletti, *Giotto. Catalogo completo*, Florence 1989.

Photographic Credits
Sergio Anelli, Milan
Elemond Archives, Milan
Foto Saporetti, Milan
Scala, Florence

An incredible visit to Italy – arriving Rome on Friday 7th February, hoping that Monsignor would be in Rome by the 14th so that we could travel to Udine by train and spend the rest of my stay with the Costanzos. After many occasions of change of dates for the proposed visit of Monsignor Causero from Tirana, it became obvious I couldn't just stay on endlessly in Rome so decided to move on to Udine. In these seven days had shopped with Elena, had lunch at Trattoria Bucca di Ryppetta, had dinner at a restaurant with Sanya and Alberto and dinner at their lovely home in via Appia Antica with the whole Petean family. # On Saturday morning I awoke very early to attend Mass at the small church of St. Anne's outside the Vatican piazza and then caught the bus to the top of the hill to the Vatican Museum (it was too cold and windy and my allergy to the cold disallowed the walk). As I slit and cross the road to the Museum (with eagerness to at last see the Sistine and a sense of regret that Monsignor could not share this long-delayed experience in hopes for his now cancelled arrival dates materializing to share the especially planned visit and viewing of the magnificent restored paintings in this gem of a salon), stand on the median, I was hit by a truck which was driving on the wrong side of the street. The whole experience is an invaluable lesson in my human frailty and my full dependence on our most compassionate provisional omnipotent God. On impact I prayed to Him and all through the nightmare of the experience and immense pain in Santos Spiritus, I prayed. The outcome was miracles upon miracles which will take volumes of paper to write about. The four broken ribs, incredible damage to chin, lips, palate and teeth plus gums (all the stitches and the partial numbness to parts of my frontal panel of my face), the awful